You come alone

you leave alone

and in between

you sing alone

so dance you must

and thrash your sword

and run - not from

but at - and toward

Are You?

So after

when thy race is done

and met there

by the setting sun

Yes

lay it down

thou's sword of weight

and there shall rest

your former fate

-the sage of K far Nahum

Legend has it...

During the reign of Tiberius, a young boy of seven or eight was orphaned in the Land of Galilee. For two days and nights he wandered dusty trails, surviving on bread scraps and water from passing travelers.

Tired, scared and dazed, the boy came upon a house on the north end of the great lake. On that third morning, from an open doorway, his eyes rose to meet those of a man who made his heart beat as never before. Somehow...

With the rising sun weaving gold among the black shadows, the boy felt himself lifted into strong, loving arms. Like a lost lamb by his shepherd. He was washed, placed in clean clothes and fed a meal of fish and figs. Later, in a room of 12 others, enfolded in the man's light, the young boy would forever recall the feelings of eternal connection.

And a presence...

Exhausted from his ordeal, the boy fell into a deep sleep. He dreamed of flying with a falcon. From that day he was cared for by parents of one of the 12 and raised in love as one of their own.

> *Whoever receives one child such as this in my name, receives me; and whoever receives me, receives not me but the one who sent me.*
> —Jesus of Nazareth

He was observant and grew wise from watching the works of these men. And a woman. Known about the great lake as Mark, he departed Capernaum at the age of 18 with gratitude, a cedar walking stick and a feather.

Over time, he refined his writing craft. In his latter years, lost souls and seekers of truth sought this *sage of Kfar Nahum* for his revelatory musings.

Mark knew he would see the man of light again. Somehow...

*...then I was with him,
as one brought up with him;
and I was his daily delight...
rejoicing in the habitable part
of his earth...*

~ Proverbs 8

Treasured

the sound
more important felt
than heard
or spoken

Older

than ancient souls
across the universe
it resonates
unbroken

And

it feels like
YES

YES

A Parable of Possibility

Copyright (c) 2022 by Gary Mark Lesley
All Rights Reserved.
No part of this publication, or it's weavings,
may be re-printed or *re-woven*
without the Master Weaver's written permission.
(Just ask.)
Cover Art & Photos: Gary Mark Lesley
Printed in the United States of America
Published by Barefoot In Paradise Lyrics
Mankato, MN
First Edition
1st Printing: 7 December, 2015
Re-Mastered Edition
1st Printing: 27 August, 2022
2nd Printing: 20 October, 2022

Earth: $10
Khumbu Valley & Rest of the Universe: Complementary

What we are
is not as we are
any more so
that what is the wine
and what is the jar

Lessons of light to share.

To illumine and clarify.
To re-connect with your very own, inner-silk.
To support and guide as you step forward.
To re-discover authentic joy, back through the divine ground, in reverence, radiance and humility.

To open ears and prepare hearts.

A return to *sage* guidance can be most helpful, as you hear, however faint, a comforting voice. And however feeble, a familiar feeling.

And engage your course to greater joy.

Delving into the mirrored reflection of your own eyes, with mind wide open, there is a deep desire to push off from the familiar lights of shore. But deep, dark waters are daunting with the swallowing waves of fear. Knowing, again, that you are a being of the sea, from birth and beyond, you will summon the faith and strength to raise the anchor. And set sail.

A bank along the River Jordan

The well-traveled man of meanings prepared to share a lesson at water's edge to a small group gathered round.

Seekers, skeptics and lost souls alike; thirsting to quench the flames of fear from life in such dark, distressing times.

Gripped in his left hand; a cedar walking stick and falcon feather bound with leather cord. A yellowed, edge-worn scroll, still rolled tight with a purple band, filled his right hand.

Words began to flow from his heart, hoping to pass through their ears and into their souls, as sweet water from a mountain spring.

You come to me now

from near and far

and ask me of things and

places and times

First I always say to you

listen

do not reach your end

pondering

of your very self

Who

am

I

There is only the one
who knows the time and place
of your final steps
and as you are
of the one
of the light
and the sun
which is of the all
I say this to all generations
and you

Therefore

be as the wise son

from before

and yet to come

and some

now among you

who begin each day

in primal union

In brightness or gloom
continually affirming
to the eternal query
posed to their soul

the one answer

the divine confirmation

Yes

Thank you

I am

For blessed

is the dewy morning ground

upon the soles of their feet

rising lightly

upward to heaven

inward to being

and centerpiece upon the

table of inquiry

weightless and free

Yes

Thank you
I am

Now when your day is

complete

and you retire

for evening's rest

as your feet

leave the ground

for the bed

of your soul's repose

With inward eyes to heaven
looking out to sea
upon the waves
of your heart

it's never too late

pray do not wait
and offer with awe

Yes

Thank you
I am

Within you

is the seal

of the inquisitioner

and you know this

to be true

even if you feign a blind eye

or a deaf ear

The anaconda looms

as a noose

to coil about your neck

constricting your very life

only to release you

un-dead

falling for eternity

through the frozen fire

of black silence

The muffled emptiness
of aboriginal abyss

from a life left only
of referred existence

unable to resonate
with the universe
nor the illuminations of
the one

That one

who casts the true light

upon the gate

and those

who missed it

with eyes wide open

their robbers' minds

denied

Know

vain as the effort

to touch the fingerprints

of your very soul

Sobering is the plea

that arrives late

to the master

that you must resolve

Who am I

I say to you again

listen

observe the universe

of

Yes

Align and harmonize with the felt resonance of

Yes

And that is why

we have come together

so you too

may come to know

through the simplest

of verse that in the end

as the beginning

wise who listened

No words drawn
into their ash

Their offering
streams ahead
as shimmering gossamer

Endless kindling strings
upon summer winds
buoyed
in eternal reverence

breathing in
with thanks
as your soul's cradle rocks

breathing out
with Yes
as your sailing ship docks

Your grip certain
as you move aside
the silken curtain

the taking

the giving

your awakened soul

you are living

So now
as you ponder
these lessons of life
seeing I Am
as you are

Realization
no true separation
existing between you
and your star

For when

the waters of Atlantis

flow through your veins

and

the constellation of Sirius

scintillates about your neck

as your own jewels

Then

you become one

with thou art

and

you perceive all things

as limitless

and sacred

For arise
a gift glowing
bathed in gold light
rests top a fence post
for thee

A holy connection
your soul now embraces
enjoined into one you
and me

> But ask now
> and they shall teach thee...
> the fowls of the air
> they shall tell thee...
> in all these
> the hand of the Lord
> and the breath of all mankind...
> with him is wisdom and strength
> and understanding.
>
> -Book of Job

So

Who do you say you are?

You Know

Yes
you are a gift
of wisdom and light
infused throughout your soul

The inner silk

there to weave

new webs of life

to anchor and display

the presence

of your essence

Each day rise
with reverence
flowing upward
from the first footprints
of your dawn

a soothing force
new-ancient presence of
Yes
feel it resonate
within and without

Pray

I am   I be   I ring
in light and harmony
to climb
the mountain
live
in the valley
flow
like water
and soar

for I know who you are
Yes
it's possible
follow me
into the midst
of a crooked
and twisted generation
and shine
as a light in the world

> My friends
> until we share the divine ground
> once again
> ~blessings and peace~

He ended with a reverent bow and the people politely departed. Some were lifted and some shook their heads with disappointment. It was always hard to know if the message had gotten through to any of them. As he was turning to go, a young woman of 12 or 13 approached. His heart felt the presence of a wise soul and the words: *Who ever receives one child such as this...*

Sage, I would be most grateful if you would teach me the prayer from your lesson? For I too wish to share it with others who need to know there is a way to greater happiness. I must also let my mother know I have followed her wishes to come see and hear you. She speaks much like you, with words of hope... and that it's always possible. And that someday we would meet.

A familiar sparkle gleamed from the girl's eyes; a light Mark had not seen since the day he left Kfar Nahum years ago. He smiled at her, exhaled slowly and spoke a word that, somehow, she felt resonate deep within her heart: *Yes.*

What inspires you toward
fires you forward
What resonates your insights
manifests your delights
And she - who challenged, sings
takes to flight
upon God's own wings

*Yes... Know... It's Possible.
Now Pass it on...*

The true essence of this simple parable is about sharing possibilities, starting with you!

After taking in the light and wisdom of these words, allowing them to be infused into your heart and soul and mind, consider passing this humble book on...

...to another soul that needs to know...
It's Possible.

Yes!

Make a small note in your own handwriting of the I AM prayer.

It's yours now, anyway!

Here's to You... and Yes!

From: *Where:*   *Date:*

~ We are all Connected ~

Minnesotan Gary Mark Lesley is the author of illuminating poetry and prose on topics involving *Contemplative Awareness, Inspiration* and *Spiritual Growth.* Through the harmonies of duality and resonating with the world of *conscious presence*, Gary's lyrical style helps reflect the sacred in both the inanimate nature and the sentient. Residing in Mankato, MN and active with his alma mater Minnesota State University, you may find him working on his next project along the shores of Lake Chapala in Mexico or in Khumjung Village near the base of Mt. Everest in Nepal. He is an entrepreneur, mentor, endurance athlete, aviator, photo journalist, junior anthropologist and *still...* a Vikings fan.

For more about Gary, his blog, and future projects
visit his website at: GossamerTrails.com

Interested in having Gary speak or present?
email him directly at: gmlesley@gmail.com

Watch for Gary's next work:

Journey of the 7 Mirrors
-A Return to Zenith Station-

Taking to heart advice from renowned mythologist Joseph Campbell, to *transcend the transparent and follow your bliss,* Gary Lesley sets out for ancient lands, indigenous people and a sacred Camino... or two. From Mexico; the land of obsidiana, the Plumed Serpent and midnight zephyrs, Lesley is led into the rarefied, azure air of Sagarmatha and the Goddess Mother of the Himalayas; calling down from *the ceiling* of the world. *Om mane padme hum...*

A universal ticket is on-call for you at **Zenith Station**; the highest terminal on earth, where arrival and departure gates merge. And the destination? *To the one true summit.* Reflected in a **Journey of** Sherpa and Sir Hillary... and **the 7 Mirrors**.

To grand daughters Jade, Jasmine and Jayla:
You can not yet read, but when you are able,
I hope you will already know: *It's possible...*